BUSINESS ENVIRONMENT,

MARKET RESEARCH

AND

BRAND MANAGEMENT

:: Author ::

KINCHIT PARESHBHAI SHAH

(M.COM., C.A. – CPT., P.G.D.T.P(Gold Medalist)., SLET)

PUBLISHED BY

Hemchadracharya International Publishing House
HQ. At & Po. Chaveli., Ta- Chansma,
Dist- Patan, North Gujarat, India, Asia.
www.iphouseindia.com

First Publication: 23TH JANUARY, 2015

ISBN:- 978-15-08712-12-1

Price: Rs.750/- INDIA
      $ 15 OUTSIDE INDIA

PUBLISHED BY

**Hemchadracharya International Publishing House
HQ. At & Po. Chaveli., Ta- Chansma,
Dist- Patan, North Gujarat, India, Asia.
www.iphouseindia.com**

Dedicated
to
my
Parents

BUSINESS ENVIRONMENT
Meaning of Business Environment

The term 'business environment' means the sum total of all individuals, institutions and other forces that are outside the control of a business enterprise but that may affect its performance. As one writer has put it– "Just take the universe, subtract from it the subset that represents the organisation, and the remainder is environment". Thus, the economic, social, political, technological and other forces which operate outside a business enterprise are part of its environment. So also, the individual consumers or competing enterprises as well as the governments, consumer groups, competitors, courts, media and other institutions working outside an enterprise constitute its environment. The important point is that these individuals, institutions and forces are likely to influence the performance of a business enterprise although they happen to exist outside its boundaries. For example, changes in government's economic policies, rapid technological developments, political uncertainty, changes in fashions and tastes of consumers and increased competition in the market — all influence the working of a business enterprise in important ways. Increase in taxes by government can make things expensive to buy.

Technological improvements may render existing products obsolete. Political uncertainty may create fear in the minds of investors. Changes in fashions and tastes of consumers may shift demand in the market from existing products to new ones. Increased competition in the market may reduce profit margins of firms.

On the basis of the foregoing discussion, it can be said business environment, has the following features:

(i) Totality of external forces: Business environment is the sum total of all things external to business firms and, as such, is aggregative in nature.

(ii) Specific and general forces: Business environment includes both specific and general forces. Specific forces (such as investors, customers, competitors and suppliers) affect individual enterprises directly and immediately in their day-to-day working. General forces (such as social, political, legal and technological conditions) have impact on all business enterprises and thus may affect an individual firm only indirvectly.

(iii) Inter-relatedness: Different elements or parts of business environment are closely inter-related. For example, increased life expectancy of people and increased awareness for health care have increased the demand for many health products and services like diet Coke, fat-free cooking oil, and health resorts. New health products and services have, in turn, changed people's life styles.

(iv) Dynamic nature: Business environment is dynamic in that it keeps on changing whether in terms of technological improvement, shifts in consumer preferences or entry of new competition in the market.

(v) Uncertainty: Business environment is largely uncertain as it is very difficult to predict future happenings, especially when environment changes are taking place too frequently as in the case of information technology or fashion industries.

(vi) Complexity: Since business environment consists of numerous interrelated and dynamic cond-itions or forces which arise from different sources, it becomes difficult to comprehend at once what exactly constitutes a given environment. In other words, environment is a complex pheno-menon that is relatively easier to understand in parts but difficult to grasp in its totality. For example, it may be difficult to know the extent of the relative impact of the social, economic, political, technological or legal factors on change in demand of a product in the market.

(vii) Relativity: Business environment is a relative concept since it differs from country to country and even region to region. Political conditions in the USA, for instance, differ from those in China or Pakistan. Similarly, demand for sarees may be fairly high in India whereas it may be almost non-existent in France.

Importance of Business Environment

Just like human beings, business enterprises do not exist in isolation. Each business firm is not an island unto itself; it exists, survives and grows within the context of the element and forces of its environment. While an individual firm is able to do little to change or control these forces, it has no alternative to responding or adapting according to them. A good understanding of environment by business managers enables them not only to identify and evaluate, but also to react to the forces external to their firms. The importance of business environment and its understanding by managers can be appreciated if we consider the following facts:

(i) It enables the firm to identify opportunities and getting the first mover advantage: Opportunities refer to the positive external trends or changes that will help a firm to improve its performance. Environment provides numerous opportunities for business success. Early identification of opportunities helps an enterprise to be the first to exploit them instead of losing them to competitors. For example, Maruti Udyog became the leader in the small car market because it was the first to recognise the need for small cars in an environment of rising petroleum prices and a large middle class population in India.

(ii) It helps the firm to identify threats and early warning signals: Threats refer to the external environment trends and changes that will hinder a firm's performance. Besides opportunities, environment happens to be the source of many threats. Environmental awareness can help managers to identify various threats on time and serve as an early warning signal. For example, if an Indian firm finds that a foreign multinational is entering the Indian market with new substitutes, it should act as a warning signal. On the basis of this information, the Indian firms can prepare themselves to meet the threat by adopting such measures as improving the quality of the product, reducing cost of the production, engaging in aggressive advertising, and so on.

(iii) It helps in tapping useful resources: Environment is a source of various resources for running a business. To engage in any type of activity, a business enterprise assembles various resources called inputs like finance, machines, raw materials, power and water, labour, etc., from its environment including financiers, government and suppliers. They decide to provide these resources with their own expectations to get something in return from the enterprise. The business enterprise supplies the environment with its outputs such as goods and services for customers, payment of taxes to government, return on financial investment to investors and so on. Because the enterprise depends on the environment as a source of inputs or resources and as an outlet for outputs, it only makes sense that the enterprise designs policies that allow it to get the resources that it needs so that it can convert those resources into outputs that the environment desires. This can be done better by understanding what the environment has to offer.

(iv) It helps in coping with rapid changes: Today's business environment is getting increasingly dynamic where changes are taking place at a fast pace. It is not the fact of change itself that is so important as the pace of change. Turbulent market conditions, less brand loyalty, divisions and sub-divisions (fragmentation) of markets, more demanding customers, rapid changes in technology and intense global competition are just a few of the images used to describe today's business environment. All sizes and all types of enterprises are facing increasingly dynamic environment. In order to effectively cope with these significant changes, managers must understand and examine the environment and develop suitable courses of action.

(v) It helps in assisting in planning and policy formulation: Since environment is a source of both opportunities and threats for a business enterprise, its understanding and analysis can be the basis for deciding the future course of action (planning) or training guidelines for decision making (policy). For instance, entry of new players in the market, which means more competition may make an enterprise think afresh about how to deal with the situation.

(vi) It helps in improving performance: The final reason for understanding business environment relates to whether or not it really makes a difference in the performance of an enterprise. The answer is that it does appear to make a difference. Many studies reveal that the future of an enterprise is closely bound up with what is happening in the environment. And, the enterprises that continuously monitor their environment and adopt suitable business practices are the ones which not only improve their present performance but also continue to succeed in the market for a longer period.

Dimensions of Business Environment

Dimensions of, or the factors constituting the business environment include economic, social, technological, political and legal conditions which are considered relevant for decision-making and improving the performance of an enterprise. In contrast to the specific environment, these factors explain the general environment which mostly influences many enterprises at the same time. However, management of every enterprise can benefit from being aware of these dimensions instead of being disinterested in them. For instance, scientific research has discovered a technology that makes it possible to produce an energy efficient light bulb that lasts at least twenty times as long as a standard bulb. Senior managers in the lighting divisions at General Electric and Phillips recognised that this discovery had the potential to significantly affect their unit growth and profitability, So they have carefully followed the progress on this research and profitably used its findings. discussion of the various factors constituting the general environment of business is given below:

(i) Economic Environment: Interest rates, inflation rates, changes in disposable income of people, stock market indices and the value of rupee are some of the economic factors that can affect management practices in a business enterprise. Short and long term interest rates significantly affect the demand for product and services. For example, in case of construction companies and automobile manufacturers, low longer-term rates are beneficial because they result in increased spending by consumers for buying homes and cars on borrowed money. Similarly, a rise in the disposable income of people due to increase in the gross domestic product of a country creates increasing demand for products. High inflation rates generally result in constraints on business enterprises as they increase the various costs of business such as the purchase of raw materials or machinery and payment of wages and salaries to employees. and non-discriminatory employment practices. Social trends present various opportunities and threats to business enterprises. For example, the health-and-fitness trend has become popular among large number of urban dwellers. This has created a demand for products like organic food, diet soft drinks, gyms, bottled (mineral) water and food supplements. This trend has, however, harmed business in other industries like dairy processing, tobacco and liquor.

(iii)Technological Environment: Technological environment includes forces relating to scientific improvements and innovations which provide new ways of producing goods and services and new methods and techniques of operating a business. For example, recent technological, advances in computers and electronics have modified the ways in

(ii) Social Environment: The social environment of business include the social forces like customs and traditions, values, social trends, society's expectations from business, etc. Traditions define social practices that have lasted for decades or even centuries. For example, the celebration of Diwali, Id, Christmas, and Guru Parv in India provides significant financial opportunities for greetings card companies, sweets or confectionery manufacturers, tailoring outlets and many other related business. Values refer to concepts that a society holds in high esteem. In India, individual freedom, social justice, equality of opportunity and national integration are examples of major values cherished by all of us. In business terms, these values translate into freedom of choice in the market, business's responsibility towards the society

Attitudes towards product innovations, lifestyles, occupational distribution and consumer preferences

Concern with quality of life

Life expectancy

Expectations from the workforce

Shifts in the presence of women in the workforce

Birth and death rates

Population shifts

Educational system and literacy rates

Consumption habits

Composition of family

Major Elements of Social Environment

Fashion industry

(shifts towards formal wear)

Food habits

(shift towards packed food)

Electronic gadgets (increase in demand of these gadgets)

Cosmetic industry (increase in demand)

SOCIAL ENVIRONMENT

Contact any ten families known to you. Find out the changes in their consumption habits over the last five years.

Analyse the impact of these changes on the working of business enterprises.

Impact of shifts with the presence of women in the workforce Because of technological advancement, it has become possible to book railway tickets through Internet from home, office etc..

Indian Railway Catering and Tourism Corporation ltd.

(A Government of India Enterprise)

E-TICKET BOOKING ON THIS WEBSITE - A GUIDE

Register as an individual. Registration is FREE.

Login by entering your user name and password.

The 'Plan my travel and Book tickets' page appears.

Use 'HELP' option for any help required to book tickets.

Fill in the details, by following the guidelines given below.

which companies advertise their products. It is common now to see CD-ROM's, computerised information kiosks, and Internet/ World Wide Web multimedia pages highlighting the virtues of products. Similarly, retailers have direct links with suppliers who replenish stocks when needed. Manufacturers have flexible manufacturing systems. Airline companies have Internet and World Wide Web pages where customers can look for flight times, destinations and fares and book their tickets online. In addition, continuing innovations in different scientific and engineering fields such as lasers, robotics, biotechnology, food preservatives, medicine, telecommunication and synthetic fuels have provided numerous opportunities and threats for many different enterprises. Shifts in demand from vaccum tubes to transistors, from steam locomotives to dieseland electric engines, from fountain pens to ballpoint, from propeller airplanes to jets, and from typewriters to computer based word processors, have all been responsible and creating new business.

(iv)Political Environment: Political environment includes political conditions such as general stability and peace in the country and specific attitudes that elected government representatives hold towards business. The significance of political conditions in business success lies in the predictability of business activities under stable political conditions. On the other hand, there may be uncertainty of business activities due to political unrest and threats to law and order. Political stability,

The Constitution of the country

Prevailing political system

The degree of politicisation of business and economic issues

Dominant ideologies and values of major political parties

The nature and profile of political leadership and thinking of political personalities

The level of political morality

Political institutions like the government and allied agencies

Political ideology and practices of the ruling party

The extent and nature of government intervention in business

The nature of relationship of our country with foreign countries

Major Elements of Political Environment

thus, builds up confidence among business people to invest in the long term projects for the growth of the economy. Political instability can shake that confidence. Similarly, the attitudes of government officials towards business may have either positive or negative impact upon business. For example, even after opening up of our economy in 1991, foreign companies found it extremely difficult to cut through the bureaucratic red tape to get permits for doing business in India. Sometimes, it took months to process even their application for the purpose. As a result these companies were discouraged from investing in our country. The situation has improved over time.

(v) Legal Environment: Legal environment includes various legislations passed by the Government administrative orders issued by government authorities, court judgments as well as the decisions rendered by various commissions and agencies at every level of the government— centre, state or local. It is imperative for the management of every enterprise to obey the law of the land. Therefore, an adequate knowledge of rules and regulations framed by the Government is a pre-requisite for better business performance. Non-compliance of laws can land the business enterprise into legal problems. In India, a working knowledge of Companies Act 1956; Industries (Development and Regulations) Act 1951; Foreign Exchange Management Act and the Imports and Exports (Control) Act 1947; Factories Act, 1948; Trade Union Act; 1926; Workmen's Compensation Act, 1923; Industrial Disputes Act, 1947, Consumer Protection Act, 1986, Competition Act, 2002 and host of such other legal enactments as amended from time to time by the Parliament, is important for doing business.

Impact of legal environment can be illustrated with the help of government regulations to protect consumer's interests. For example, the advertisement of alcoholic beverages is prohibited. Advertisements, including packets of cigarettes carry the statutory warning 'Cigarette smoking is injurious to health'. Similarly, advertisements of baby food must necessarily inform the potential buyer that mothers milk is the best. All these regulations are required to be followed by advertisers.

Economic Environment in India

The economic environment in India consists of various macro-level factors related to the means of production and distribution of wealth which have an impact on business and industry. These include:

(a) Stage of economic development of the country.

(b) The economic structure in the form of mixed economy which recognises the role of both public and private sectors.

(c) Economic policies of the Government, including industrial, mone-tary and fiscal policies.

(d) Economic planning, including five year plans, annual budgets, and so on.

(e) Economic indices, like national income, distribution of income, rate and growth of GNP, per capita income, disposal personal income, rate of savings and investments, value of exports and imports, balance of payments, and so on.

(f) Infrastructural factors, such as, financial institutions, banks,modes of transportation communication facilities, and so on. Business enterprises in India do realise the importance and impact of the economic environment on their working. Almost all annual company reports presented by their chairpersons devote considerable attention to the general economic environment prevailing in the country and an assessment of its impact on their companies.

The economic environment of business in India has been steadily changing mainly due to the government policies. At the time of Independence:

(a) The Indian economy was mainly agricultural and rural in character;

(b) About 70% of the working population
was employed in agriculture;

(c) About 85% of the population was living in the villages;

(d) Production was carried out using irrational, low productivity technology;

(e) Communicable diseases were widespread, mortality rates were high. These was no good public health system.

In order to solve economic problems of our country, the government took several steps including control by the State of certain industries, central planning and reduced importance of the private sector. The main objectives of India's development plans were:

(a) Initiate rapid economic growth to raise the standard of living, reduce unemployment and poverty;

(b) Become self-reliant and set up a strong industrial base with emphasis on heavy and basic industries;

(c) Reduce inequalities of income and wealth;

(d) Adopt a socialist pattern of development — based on equality and prevent exploitation of man by man.

In accordance with the economic planning, the government gave a lead role to the public sector for

Major elements of the crisis situation which led the Government of India to announce economic reform were:

n A serious fiscal crisis in which the fiscal deficit reached the level of 6.6 per cent of GDP in 1990-91.n Heavy internal debt which rose to about 50 per cent of GDP with interest payments draining about 39 per cent of total revenue collections of the central government.

Low GNP growth rate which fell to 1.4 per cent from the peak level of 10.5 per cent in 1988-89 (at 1980-81 prices).

Low overall agricultural production, foodgrain production and industrial production showed negative growth rates of –2.8 per cent, –5.3 per cent and –0.1 per cent respectively.

Soaring inflation rate based both on wholesale price index and consumer price index (for industrial workers) at 13-14 per cent.

Shrinkage of foreign trade, imports (in $ terms) fell by 19.4 per cent and exports by 1.5 per cent.

Depreciation of rupee by 26.7 per cent vis-à-vis US dollars.

Fall of foreign exchange reserves to such a low level that they were barely adequate to meet the import requirements of a few weeks.

Non-resident Indians (NRIs) were withdrawing their deposits at an alarmingly high rate.

The confidence of the international financial institutions

was badly shaken and in just over a year its creditworthiness rating fell from AAA to BB+

(put on credit watch).

The country was on the verge of defaulting on international financial obligations and the situation warranted immediate policy action to save the situation. In May 1991, the Government had to lease 20 tones of gold out of its stock to the State Bank of India to enable it to sell the gold with repurchase option after six months. In addition, Reserve Bank of India was allowed to pledge 47 tones of gold to the Bank of England to raise a loan of $600 million.

Crisis of June 1991

Infrastructure industries whereas the private sector was broadly given the responsibility of developing consumer goods industry. At the same time, the government imposed several restrictions, regulations and controls on the working of private sector enterprises. India's experience with economic planning has delivered mixed results. In 1991 the economy faced a serious foreign exchange crisis, high government deficit and a rising trend of prices despite bumper crops.

As a part of economic reforms, the Government of India announced a new industrial policy in July 1991.

The broad features of this policy were as follows:

(a) The Government reduced the number of industries under compulsory licensing to six.

(b) Many of the industries reserved for the public sector under the earlier policy, were dereserved. The role of the public sector was limited only to four industries of strategic importance.

(c) Disinvestment was carried out in case of many public sector industrial enterprises.

(d) Policy towards foreign capital was liberalised. The share of foreign equity participation was increased and in many activities 100 per cent Foreign Direct Investment (FDI) was permitted.

(e) Automatic permission was now granted for technology agreements with foreign companies.

(f) Foreign Investment Promotion Board (FIPB) was set up to promote and channelise foreign investment in India.

Appropriate measures were taken to remove obstacles in the way of growth and expansion of industrial units of large industrial houses. Small-scale sector was assured all help and accorded due recognition.

In essence, this policy has sought to liberate industry from the shackles of the licensing system (liberalisation), drastically reduce the role of the public sector (privatisation) and encourage foreign private participation in India's industrial development (globalisation).

Liberalisation: The economic reforms that were introduced were aimed at liberalising the Indian business and industry from all unnecessary controls and restrictions. They signalled the end of the licence-pemit-quota raj. Liberalisation of the Indian industry has taken place with respect to:

(i) abolishing licensing requirement in most of the industries except a short list,

(ii) freedom in deciding the scale of business activities i.e., no restrictions on expansion or contraction of business activities,

(iii) removal of restrictions on the movement of goods and services,

(iv) freedom in fixing the prices of goods services,

(v) reduction in tax rates and lifting of unnecessary controls over the economy,

(vi) simplifying procedures for imports and experts, and

(vii) making it easier to attract foreign capital and technology to India.

Privatisation: The new set of economic reforms aimed at giving greater role to the private sector in the nation building process and a reduced role

to the public sector. This was a reversal

Some of the early major steps taken to manage the economic crisis were the following:

Fiscal correction aimed at reducing fiscal deficit by about Rs. 7,700 crore in

1991-92 (compared to 1990-91);

Announcement of New Industry Policy in July 1991 seeking to deregulate the industry with the objective of promoting the growth of a more competitive and efficient industrial economy;

Abolition of industrial licensing for all industrial projects except 18 industries of high strategic and environmental importance and with high import content. About 80 per cent of the industries were delicensed;

Amendment of the MRTP Act to eliminate the need for prior approval of the Central Government by large companies for capacity expansion, diversification and merger and amalgamation.

Nine areas in basic and core industries earlier reserved for the public sector were opened to the private sector;

Limit of foreign equity holding raised from 40 per cent to 51 per cent in a wide range of priority industries;

Foreign Investment Promotion Board (FIPB) established to negotiate proposals from large international firms and expedite clearances of the investment proposals;

Rupee devaluation by 18 per cent during July 1-3, 1991 supported by a standby credit of $2.3 billion from the IMP over a 20 months period negotiated in October 1991;

Negotiation of $500 million Structural Adjustment Loan from the World Bank in April 1992 and a loan totalling SDR 1.3 billion from the International Monetory Fund (IMF) between January-September 1991;

Introduction of India Development Bond Scheme and Immunity Scheme for repatriation of funds held abroad in October 1991, under which more than $2 billion were mobilised during 1991-92;

Bringing back of gold earlier pledged to the Bank of England and the Bank of Japan;

Continuance of the measures of import control and credit squeeze;

Administered licensing of imports replaced by freely tradeable import entitlements (called Eximscrips) linked to export earnings. The measure was expected to introduce self-balancing mechanism in India's foreign trade;

Introduction of Liberalised Exchange Rate Management System (LERMS) under which a dual exchange rate system was established, one rate being effectively floated in the market; and

Import licensing in most capital goods, raw materials, intermediates and components eliminated. Advance Licensing System considerably simplified.

The initial series of measures set the tone for the future economic reforms. Any of the measures taken above was continued to form a part of the ongoing reform process.

Early Crisis Met : Reform Measures

Of the development strategy pursued so far by Indian planners. To achieve this, the government redefined the role of the public sector in the New Industrial Policy of 1991, adopted the policy of planned disinvestments of the public sector and decided to refer the loss making and sick enterprises to the Board of Industrial and Financial Reconstruction. The term disinvestments used here means transfer in the public sector enterprises to the private sector. It results in dilution of stake of the Government in the public enterprise. If there is dilution of Government ownership beyond 51 percent, it would result in transfer of ownership and management of the enterprise to the private sector.

Globalisation: Globalisation means the integration of the various economies of the world leading towards the emergence of a cohesive global economy. Till 1991, the Government of India had followed a policy of strictly regulating imports in value and volume terms. These regulations were with respect to (a) licensing of imports, (b) tariff restrictions and (c) quantitative restrictions. The new economic reforms aimed at trade liberalisation were directed towards import liberalisation, export promotion through rationalisation of the tariff structure and reforms with respect to foreign exchange so that the country does not remain isolated from the rest of the world. Globalisation involves an increased level of interaction and interdependence among the various nations of the global economy. Physical geographical gap or political

A truly global economy implies a boundaryless world where there is:

(i) Free flow of goods and services across nations;

(ii) Free flow of capital across nations;

(iii) Free flow of information and technology;

(iv) Free movement of people across borders;

(v) A common acceptable mechanism for the settlement of disputes;

(vi) A global governance perspective.

boundaries no longer remain barriers for a business enterprise to serve a customer in a distant geographical market. This has been made possible by the rapid advancement in technology and liberal trade policies by Governments. Through the policy of 1991, the government of India moved the country to this globalisation pattern.

Impact of Government Policy Changes on Business and Industry

The policy of liberalisation, privatisation and globalisation of the Government has made a significant impact on the working of enterprises in business and industry. The Indian corporate sector has come face-to-face with several challenges due to government policy changes. These challenges can be explained as follows:

(i) Increasing competition: As a result of changes in the rules of industrial licensing and entry of foreign firms, competition for Indian firms has increased especially in service industries like telecommunications, airlines, banking, insurance, etc. which were earlier in the public sector.

(ii) More demanding customers: Customers today have become more demanding because they are well-informed. Increased competition in the market gives the customers wider choice in purchasing better quality of goods and services.

(iii)Repidly changing technological environment: Increased competition forces the firms to develop new ways to survive and grow in the market. New technologies make it possible to improve machines, process, products and services. The rapidly changing technological environment creates tough challenges before smaller firms.

(iv) Necessity for change: In a regulated environment of pre-1991 era, the firms could have relatively stable policies and practices. After 1991, the market forces have become turbulent as a result of which the enterprises have to continuously modify their operations.

(v) Need for developing human resource: Indian enterprises have suffered for long with inadequately trained personnel.

The new market conditions require people with higher competence and greater commitment. Hence the need for developing human resources.

(vi) Market orientation: Earlier firms used to produce first and go to the market for sale later. In other words, they had production oriented marketing operations. In a fast changing world, there is a shift to market orientation in as much as the firms have to study and analyse the market first and produce goods accordingly.

Meaning of business environment: The term business environment means the totality of all individuals, institutions and other forces that are outside a business but that potentially affect its performance. Business environment can be characterised in terms of

(a) totality of external forces

(b) specific and general forces

(c) inter-relatedness

(d) dynamic nature

(e) uncertainty

(f) complexity

(g) relativity

Importance of business environment:

Business environment and its understanding are important for (i) enabling the identification of opportunities and getting the first mover advantage, (ii) helping in the identification of threats and early warning signals, (iii) coping with the rapid changes, (v) assisting in planning and policy and

(vi) improving the performance.

(vii) Loss of budgetary support to the public sector: The central government's budgetary support for financing the public sector outlays has declined over the years. The public sector undertakings have realised that, in order to survive and grow, they will have to be more efficient and generate their own resources for the purpose.

On the whole, the impact of Government policy changes particularly in respect of liberalisation, privatisation and globalisation has been positive as the Indian business and industry has shown great resilience in dealing with the new economic order. Indian enterprises have developed strategies and adopted business processes and procedures to meet the challenge of competition. They have become more customer-focused and adopted measures to improve customer relationship and satisfaction.

Elements of business environment: Business environment consists of five important dimensions including economic, social, technological, political and legal.

Economic environment includes such factors as interest rates, inflation rates, changes in disposable income of people, stock market indexes and the value of rupee.

Social environment includes social forces like traditions, values, social trends, society's expectations of business, and so on.

Technological environment includes forces relating to scientific improvements and innovations which provide new ways of producing goods and services and new methods and techniques of operating a business.

Political environment includes political conditions such as general stability and peace in the country and specific attitudes that elected government representatives hold toward business.

Legal environment includes various legislations passed by the government, administrative orders issued by government authorities, court judgments as well as decisions rendered by various commissions and agencies at every level of the government center, state or local.

Economic environment in India: The economic environment in India consists of various macro-level factors related to the means of production and distribution of wealth which have an impact on business and industry. The economic environment of business in India has been steadily changing since Independence mainly due to government policies. In order to solve economic problems of our country at the time of Independence, the government took several steps including control by the state of key industries, central planning and reduced importance of the private sector. These steps delivered mixed results until 1991 when Indian economy happened to face serious foreign exchange crisis, high government deficit and a rising trend of prices despite bumper crops.

Liberalisation, privatisation and globalisation: As a part of economic reforms, the Government of India announced a new industrial policy in July 1991 which sought to liberate the industry from the shackles of the licensing system (liberalisation), drastically reduce the role of the public sector (privatisation) and encourage foreign private participation in industrial development (globalisation).

Meaning and Scope of Marketing Research

According to *American Marketing Association*, "Marketing Research is the function that links the consumer, customer and public to the marketer through information-information used to identify and define marketing opportunities and problems, generate, refine and evaluate marketing actions; monitor marketing performance; and improve understanding of marketing as a process."

Marketing Research is systematic problem analysis, model building and fact finding for the purpose of important decision making and control in the marketing of goods and services.

Marketing Research is a well-planned, systematic process which implies that it needs planning at all the stages. It uses scientific method. It is an objective process as it attempts to provide accurate authentic information. Marketing Research is sometimes defined as the application of scientific method in the solution of marketing problems.

Marketing Research plays a very significant role in identifying the needs of customers and meeting them in best possible way. The main task of Marketing Research is systematic gathering and analysis of information.

Before we proceed further, it is essential to clarify the relationship and difference between Marketing Research and Marketing Information System (MIS). Whatever information are generated by Marketing Research from internal sources, external sources, marketing intelligence agencies-consist the part of MIS.

MIS is a set of formalized procedures for generating, analyzing, storing and distributing information to marketing decision makers on an ongoing basis.

1. While Marketing Research is done with a specific purpose in mind with information being generated when it is conducted, MIS information is generated continuously.

2. MIS is continuous entity while Marketing Research is a ad-hoc system.

3. While in Marketing Research information is for specific purpose, so it is not rigid; in MIS information is more rigid and structured.

Marketing Research is essential for strategic market planning and decision making. It helps a firm in identifying what are the market opportunities and constraints, in developing and implementing market strategies, and in evaluating the effectiveness of marketing plans.

Marketing Research is a growing and widely used business activity as the sellers need to know more about their final consumers but are generally widely separated from those consumers. Marketing Research is a necessary link between marketing decision makers and the markets in which they operate.

Marketing Research includes various important principles for generating information which is useful to managers. These principles relate to the timeliness and importance of data, the significance of defining objectives cautiously and clearly, and the need to avoid conducting research to support decisions already made.

Marketing Research is of use to the following:-

1. Producers

    a. To know about his product potential in the market vis-à-vis the total product;

    b. New Products;

    c. Various brands;

    d. Pricing;

e. Market Structures and selection of product strategy, etc.

2. Business and Government

Marketing Research helps businesses and government in focusing attention on the complex nature of problems faced by them. For example:

a. Determination of Gross National Product; Price indices, and per capita income;

b. Expenditure levels and budgeting;

c. Agricultural Pricing;

d. The economic policies of Government; and

e. Operational and planning problems of business and industry.

3. Market Research Agencies

Marketing Research is being used extensively by professionals to help conducting various studies in Marketing Research. Most prominent agencies being:-

a. Linta India Ltd;

b. British Market Research Bureau (BMRB);

c. Hindustan Thompson Associate Ltd;

d. eSurveysPro.com;

e. MARG

4. Managers

Limitations of Marketing Research

Following are the main limitations of Marketing Research:

- Marketing Research (MR) is not an exact science though it uses the techniques of science. Thus, the results and conclusions drawn upon by using MR are not very accurate.

- The results of MR are very vague as MR is carried out on consumers, suppliers, intermediaries, etc. who are humans. Humans have a tendency to behave artificially when they know that they are being observed. Thus, the consumers and respondents upon whom the research is carried behave artificially when they are aware that their attitudes, beliefs, views, etc are being observed.

- MR is not a complete solution to any marketing issue as there are many dominant variables between research conclusions and market response.

- MR is not free from bias. The research conclusions cannot be verified. The reproduction of the same project on the same class of respondents give different research results.

- Inappropriate training to researchers can lead to misapprehension of questions to be asked for data collection.

- Many business executives and researchers have ambiguity about the research problem and it's objectives. They have limited experience of the notion of the decision-making process. This leads to carelessness in research and researchers are not able to do anything real.

- There is less interaction between the MR department and the main research executives. The research department is in segregation. This all makes research ineffective.

- MR faces time constraint. The firms are required to maintain a balance between the requirement for having a broader perspective of customer needs and the need for quick decision making so as to have competitive advantage.

- Huge cost is involved in MR as collection and processing of data can be costly. Many firms do not have the proficiency to carry wide surveys for collecting primary data, and might not also able to hire specialized market experts and research agencies to collect primary data.

Thus, in that case, they go for obtaining secondary data that is cheaper to obtain.

- MR is conducted in open marketplace where numerous variables act on research settings.

Data Collection in Marketing Research

Data Collection in Marketing Research is a detailed process in which a planned search for all relevant data is made by researcher.

Types of Data

1. **Primary Data-** Primary data is the data which is collected first hand specially for the purpose of study. It is collected for addressing the problem at hand. Thus, primary data is original data collected by researcher first hand.

2. **Secondary data-** Secondary data is the data that have been already collected by and readily available from other sources. Such data are cheaper and more quickly obtainable than the primary data and also may be available when primary data can not be obtained at all.

Data Collection Methods

1. **Qualitative Research-** Qualitative Research is generally undertaken to develop an initial understanding of the

problem. It is non statistical in nature. It uses an inductive method, that is, data relevant to some topics are collected and grouped into appropriate meaningful categories. The explanations are emerged from the data itself. It is used in exploratory research design and descriptive research also. Qualitative data comes into a variety of forms like interview transcripts; documents, diaries and notes made while observing. There are two main methods for collecting Qualitative data

a. Direct Collection Method-When the data is collected directly, it makes use of disguised method. Purpose of data collection is not known. This method makes use of-

    i.   Focus Groups

    ii. Depth Interview

    iii. Case Study

b. Indirect Collection-Method

    i.   Projective Techniques

2. **Quantitative Research**-Quantitative Research quantifies the data and generalizes the results from the sample to the population. In Quantitative Research, data can be colleted by two methods

1. Survey Method

2. Observation Method

Focus Groups

Focus groups are also known as group interviews or group discussions. They are used to understand the attitude or behaviour of the audience. Six to twelve individuals are selected and either one or two moderators (those who lead the discussions) are selected. If there are two moderators, they will adopt opposite positions. It is the moderator who introduces the topic. Discussion is controlled through these moderators. The group is watched from adjacent rooms. There are various devices which are used to record these discussions.

Objectives of Focus Group

1. To gather primary information for research project;

2. To help developing questionnaires in terms of survey research;

3. To understand reason behind a particular phenomenon:

4. To see how people interpret certain phenomenon;

5. To test primarily ideas or plan

Steps involved in conducting Focus group

1. Define the problem

2. Select a sample

3. Determine the number of groups necessary(minimum number should be two)

4. Prepare the study mechanics. Arrange the respondents place where the focus group is to be assembled.

5. Select moderators and brief them.

6. Prepare the focus group material.

7. Conduct the session.

8. Analyze the data and prepare summary report.

Advantages of Focus Group

1. It is used to collect primary information and therefore it can conduct a pilot study also.

2. Relative cost is not much.

3. It can be conducted quickly.

4. It has flexibility.

5. Moderator can detect the opinion and certificates of those who cannot speak well by facial expression and other non verbal behaviour.

6. We can get the questionnaire filled up either before or after the discussion.

Disadvantages of Focus Group

1. It is inappropriate for gathering quantitative data.

2. Self appointed group leader may impose his /her opinion on other members. Moderators can restrict people.

3. t depends heavily on skills of moderator.

4. Respondents in the focus group may or may not represent the population from which they are drawn.

5. Recording equipments are likely to restrict respondents. Location of recording equipment is very important.

Depth Interview

They generally use small samples and also conduct direct one to one personal interviews. A detailed background is provided by the respondents and elaborate data concerning the respondents opinions, values, motivation, expression, feeling etc are obtained. Even their non-verbal expressions are observed. They take long time, therefore lengthy observations are involved.

These are conducted to customize individual responses. The questions will depend on what kind of answers are given. Even interview climate influences the respondents. The success of interviews depends on the rapport of the interviewers established with the respondents.

Advantages of Depth Interview

1. Lot of detail is provided.

2. Information obtained is comparatively more accurate.

3. Personal or intimate topic can also be discussed since the personal rapport is established between the respondent and the interviewer

Disadvantages of Depth Interview

1. It is difficult to generalize since the interviewers are non-standardized

2. Since the success depends on the interviewer, there are chances of bias.

3. Data analysis takes a lot of time.

Case study

Individual cases are taken and a detailed study of each case is done.

Advantages of Case Study

1. Accurate data is provided

2. There is detailed analysis

Disadvantages of Case Study

1. It is difficult to generalize.

2. It consumes lot of time.

3. Confidential and sensitive information may not be given.

4. Interviewer bias is there.

Projective Techniques

Projective Techniques are indirect and unstructured methods of investigation which have been developed by the psychologists and use projection of respondents for inferring about underline motives, urges or intentions which cannot be secure through direct questioning as the respondent either resists to reveal them or is unable to figure out himself. These techniques are useful in giving respondents opportunities to express their attitudes without personal embarrassment. These techniques helps the respondents to project his own attitude and feelings unconsciously on the subject under study. Thus Projective Techniques play a important role in motivational researches or in attitude surveys.

Important Projective Techniques

1. Word Association Test.

2. Completion Test.

3. Construction Techniques

4. Expression Techniques

1. **Word Association Test:** An individual is given a clue or hint and asked to respond to the first thing that comes to mind. The association can take the shape of a picture or a word. There can be many interpretations of the same thing. A list of words is given and you don't know in

which word they are most interested. The interviewer records the responses which reveal the inner feeling of the respondents. The frequency with which any word is given a response and the amount of time that elapses before the response is given are important for the researcher. For eg: Out of 50 respondents 20 people associate the word " Fair" with "Complexion".

2. **Completion Test:** In this the respondents are asked to complete an incomplete sentence or story. The completion will reflect their attitude and state of mind.

3. **Construction Test:** This is more or less like completion test. They can give you a picture and you are asked to write a story about it. The initial structure is limited and not detailed like the completion test. For eg: 2 cartoons are given and a dialogue is to written.

4. **Expression Techniques:** In this the people are asked to express the feeling or attitude of other people.

Disadvantages of Projective Techniques

1. Highly trained interviewers and skilled interpreters are needed.

2. Interpreters bias can be there.

3. It is a costly method.

4. The respondent selected may not be representative of the entire population.

Survey Method

The Survey method is the technique of gathering data by asking questions to people who are thought to have desired information. A formal list of questionnaire is prepared. Generally a non disguised approach is used. The respondents are asked questions on their demographic interest opinion.

Advantages of Survey Method

1. As compared to other methods (direct observation, experimentation) survey yield a broader range of information. Surveys are effective to produce information on socio-economic characteristics, attitudes, opinions, motives etc and to gather information for planning product features, advertising media, sales promotion, channels of distribution and other marketing variables.

2. Questioning is usually faster and cheaper that Observation.

3. Questions are simple to administer.

4. Data is reliable

5. The variability of results is reduced.

6. It is relatively simple to analyze, quote and interrelate the data obtained by survey method

Disadvantages of Survey Method

1. Unwillingness of respondents to provide information- This requires salesmanship on the part of the interviewer. The interviewer may assure that the information will be kept secret or apply the technique of offering some presents.

2. Inability of the respondents to provide information- This may be due to
   a. Lack of knowledge
   b. Lapse of memory
   c. Inability to identify their motives and provide "reasons why?" for their actions

3. Human Biases of the respondents are there, for eg: "Ego"

4. Symantec difficulties are there - it is difficult, if not impossible, to state a given question in such a way that it will mean exactly same thing to each respondent. Similarly two different wordings of the same question will frequently produce quite different results.

How to overcome the limitations of Survey Method

1. Careful framing and phrasing of questions.

2. Careful control of data gathering by employing specially trained investigators who will observe carefully report on subtle reactions of persons interviewed

3. Cautious interpretations by a clear recognition of the limitations of the data and understating of what exactly the data represents. This is especially true of responses to questions like - "What price would you be willing to pay for this product?"

4. Looking at facts in relative rather than absolute terms. For eg - A survey by a dentist team showed that the number of families in the middle income group used toothpaste taken by itself in the absolute sense, the results of the survey are in some doubt. Even though the individual group readings shall differ say for eg: for upper income group families it could be 90 %. Hence we should look at the facts in relative rather than in absolute terms

Techniques of Survey Method

There are mainly 4 methods by which we can collect data through the Survey Method

1. Telephonic Interview

2. Personal Interview

3. Mail Interview

4. Electronic Interview

1. Telephonic Interview

Telephone Interviewing stands out as the best method for gathering quickly needed information. Responses are collected from the respondents by the researcher on telephone.

Advantages of Telephonic Interview

1. It is very fast method of data collection.

2. It has the advantage over "Mail Questionnaire" of permitting the interviewer to talk to one or more persons and to clarifying his questions if they are not understood.

3. Response rate of telephone interviewing seems to be a little better than mail questionnaires

4. The quality of information is better

5. It is less costly method and there are less administration problems

Disadvantages of Telephonic Interview

6. They cant handle interview which need props

7. It cant handle unstructured interview

8. It cant be used for those questions which requires long descriptive answers

9. Respondents cannot be observed

10. People are reluctant to disclose personal information on telephone

11. People who don't have telephone facility cannot be approached

2. Personal Interviewing

It is the most versatile of the all methods. They are used when props are required along with the verbal response non-verbal responses can also be observed.

Advantages of Personal Interview

1. The person interviewed can ask more questions and can supplement the interview with personal observation.

2. They are more flexible. Order of questions can be changed

3. Knowledge of past and future is possible.

4. In-depth research is possible.

5. Verification of data from other sources is possible.

6. The information obtained is very reliable and dependable and helps in establishing cause and effect relationship very early.

Disadvantages of Personal Interview

1. It requires much more technical and administrative planning and supervision

2. It is more expensive

3. **It is time consuming**

   1. The accuracy of data is influenced by the interviewer

   2. A number of call banks may be required

   3. Some people are not approachable

4. Mail Survey

Questionnaires are send to the respondents, they fill it up and send it back.

Advantages of Mail Survey

1. It can reach all types of people.

2. Response rate can be improved by offering certain incentives.

Disadvantages of Mail Survey

1. It can not be used for unstructured study.

2. It is costly.

3. It requires established mailing list.

4. It is time consuming.

5. There is problem in case of complex questions.

5. Electronic Interview

Electronic interviewing is a process of recognizing and noting people, objects, occurances rather than asking for information. For example-When you go to store, you notice which product people like to use. The Universal Product Code (UPC) is also a method of observing what people are buying.

Advantages of Electronic Interview

1. There is no relying on willingness or ability of respondent.

2. The data is more accurate and objective.

Disadvantages of Electronic Interview

1. Attitudes can not be observed.

2. Those events which are of long duration can not be observed.

3. There is observer bias. It is not purely objective.

4. If the respondents know that they are being observed, their response can be biased.

5. It is a costly method.

Observation Method

The observation method involves human or mechanical observation of what people actually do or what events take place during a buying or consumption situation. "Information is collected by observing process at work. "The following are a few situations:-

1. Service Stations-Pose as a customer, go to a service station and observe.

2. To evaluate the effectiveness of display of Dunlop Pillow Cushions-In a departmental store, observer notes:- a) How many pass by; b) How many stopped to look at the display; c) How many decide to buy.

3. Super Market-Which is the best location in the shelf? Hidden cameras are used.

4. To determine typical sales arrangement and find out sales enthusiasm shown by various salesmen-Normally this is done by an investigator using a concealed tape-recorder.

Advantages of Observation Method

1. If the researcher observes and record events, it is not necessary to rely on the willingness and ability of respondents to report accurately.

2. The biasing effect of interviewers is either eliminated or reduced. Data collected by observation are, thus, more objective and generally more accurate.

Disadvantages of Observation Method

1. The most limiting factor in the use of observation method is the inability to observe such things such as attitudes, motivations, customers/consumers state of mind, their buying motives and their images.

2. It also takes time for the investigator to wait for a particular action to take place.

3. Personal and intimate activities, such as watching television late at night, are more easily discussed with questionnaires than they are observed.

4. Cost is the final disadvantage of observation method. Under most circumstances, observational data are more expensive to obtain than other survey data. The observer has to wait doing nothing, between events to be observed. The unproductive time is an increased cost.

Secondary Data

Secondary data is the data that have been already collected by and readily available from other sources. Such data are cheaper and more quickly obtainable than the primary data and also may be available when primary data can not be obtained at all.

Advantages of Secondary data

1. It is economical. It saves efforts and expenses.

2. It is time saving.

3. It helps to make primary data collection more specific since with the help of secondary data, we are able to make out what are the gaps and deficiencies and what additional information needs to be collected.

4. It helps to improve the understanding of the problem.

5. It provides a basis for comparison for the data that is collected by the researcher.

Disadvantages of Secondary Data

1. Secondary data is something that seldom fits in the framework of the marketing research factors. Reasons for its non-fitting are:-

    a. Unit of secondary data collection-Suppose you want information on disposable income, but the data is available on gross income. The information may not be same as we require.

    b. Class Boundaries may be different when units are same.

Before 5 Years	After 5 Years
2500-5000	5000-6000
5001-7500	6001-7000
7500-10000	7001-10000

   c. Thus the data collected earlier is of no use to you.

2. Accuracy of secondary data is not known.

3. Data may be outdated.

Evaluation of Secondary Data

Because of the above mentioned disadvantages of secondary data, we will lead to evaluation of secondary data. Evaluation means the following four requirements must be satisfied:-

1. Availability- It has to be seen that the kind of data you want is available or not. If it is not available then you have to go for primary data.

2. Relevance- It should be meeting the requirements of the problem. For this we have two criterion:-

   a. Units of measurement should be the same.

   b. Concepts used must be same and currency of data should not be outdated.

3. Accuracy- In order to find how accurate the data is, the following points must be considered: -

a. Specification and methodology used;

b. Margin of error should be examined;

c. The dependability of the source must be seen.

4. Sufficiency- Adequate data should be available.

Robert W Joselyn has classified the above discussion into eight steps. These eight steps are sub classified into three categories. He has given a detailed procedure for evaluating secondary data.

1. Applicability of research objective.

2. Cost of acquisition.

3. Accuracy of data.

Sources of Data

Sources of Primary Data

The sources of generating primary data are -

1. Observation Method

2. Survey Method

3. Experimental Method

Experimental Method

There are number of experimental designs that are used in carrying out and experiment. However, Market researchers have used 4 experimental designs most frequently. These are -

1. CRD - Completely Randomized Design

2. RBD - Randomized Block Design - The term Randomized Block Design has originated from agricultural research. In this design several treatments of variables are applied to different blocks of land to ascertain their effect on the yield of the crop. Blocks are formed in such a manner that each block contains as many plots as a number of treatments so that one plot from each is selected at random for each treatment. The production of each plot is measured after the treatment is given. These data are then interpreted and inferences are drawn by using the analysis of Variance Technique so as to know the effect of various treatments like different dozes of fertilizers, different types of irrigation etc.

3. LSD - Latin Square Design - A Latin square is one of the experimental designs which has a balanced two way classification scheme say for example - 4 X 4 arrangement. In this scheme each letter from A to D occurs only once in each row and also only once in each column. The balance arrangement, it may be noted that, will not get disturbed if any row gets changed with the other.

A B C D

$$B \quad C \quad D \quad A$$

$$C \quad D \quad A \quad B$$

$$D \quad A \quad B \quad C$$

4. The balance arrangement achieved in a Latin Square is its main strength. In this design, the comparisons among treatments, will be free from both differences between rows and columns. Thus the magnitude of error will be smaller than any other design.

5. FD - Factorial Designs - This design allows the experimenter to test two or more variables simultaneously. It also measures interaction effects of the variables and analyzes the impacts of each of the variables.

In a true experiment, randomization is essential so that the experimenter can infer cause and effect without any bias.

Sources of Secondary Data

While primary data can be collected through questionnaires, depth interview, focus group interviews, case studies, experimentation and observation; The secondary data can be obtained through

1. Internal Sources - These are within the organization

2. External Sources - These are outside the organization

Internal Sources of Data

If available, internal secondary data may be obtained with less time, effort and money than the external secondary data. In addition, they may also be more pertinent to the situation at hand since they are from within the organization. The internal sources include

1. **Accounting resources-** This gives so much information which can be used by the marketing researcher. They give information about internal factors.

2. **Sales Force Report-** It gives information about the sale of a product. The information provided is of outside the organization.

3. **Internal Experts-** These are people who are heading the various departments. They can give an idea of how a particular thing is working

4. **Miscellaneous Reports-** These are what information you are getting from operational reports.

If the data available within the organization are unsuitable or inadequate, the marketer should extend the search to external secondary data sources.

External Sources of Data

External Sources are sources which are outside the company in a larger environment. Collection of external data is more difficult because the data have much greater variety and the sources are much more numerous.

External data can be divided into following classes.

a. **Government Publications-** Government sources provide an extremely rich pool of data for the researchers. In addition, many of these data are available free of cost on internet websites. There are number of government agencies generating data. These are:

   i. Registrar General of India- It is an office which generate demographic data. It includes details of gender, age, occupation etc.

   ii. Central Statistical Organization- This organization publishes the national accounts statistics. It contains estimates of national income for several years, growth rate, and rate of major economic activities. Annual survey of Industries is also published by the CSO. It gives information about the total number of workers employed, production units, material used and value added by the manufacturer.

iii. Director General of Commercial Intelligence- This office operates from Kolkata. It gives information about foreign trade i.e. import and export. These figures are provided region-wise and country-wise.

iv. Ministry of Commerce and Industries- This ministry through the office of economic advisor provides information on wholesale price index. These indices may be related to a number of sectors like food, fuel, power, food grains etc. It also generates All India Consumer Price Index numbers for industrial workers, urban, non manual employees and cultural labourers.

v. Planning Commission- It provides the basic statistics of Indian Economy.

vi. Reserve Bank of India- This provides information on Banking Savings and investment. RBI also prepares currency and finance reports.

vii. Labour Bureau- It provides information on skilled, unskilled, white collared jobs etc.

viii. National Sample Survey- This is done by the Ministry of Planning and it provides social, economic, demographic, industrial and agricultural statistics.

ix. Department of Economic Affairs- It conducts economic survey and it also generates information on income, consumption, expenditure, investment, savings and foreign trade.

x. State Statistical Abstract- This gives information on various types of activities related to the state like - commercial activities, education, occupation etc.

b. **Non Government Publications-** These includes publications of various industrial and trade associations, such as

i. The Indian Cotton Mill Association

ii. Various chambers of commerce

iii. The Bombay Stock Exchange (it publishes a directory containing financial accounts, key profitability and other relevant matter)

iv. Various Associations of Press Media.

v. Export Promotion Council.

vi. Confederation of Indian Industries (CII)

vii. Small Industries Development Board of India

viii. Different Mills like - Woolen mills, Textile mills etc

The only disadvantage of the above sources is that the data may be biased. They are likely to colour their negative points.

c. **Syndicate Services-** These services are provided by certain organizations which collect and tabulate the marketing information on a regular basis for a number of clients who are the subscribers to these services. So the services are designed in such a way that the information suits the subscriber. These services are useful in television viewing, movement of consumer goods etc. These syndicate services provide information data from both household as well as institution.

In collecting data from household they use three approaches

    i.   Survey- They conduct surveys regarding - lifestyle, sociographic, general topics.

    ii.   Mail Diary Panel- It may be related to 2 fields - Purchase and Media.

    iii.   Electronic Scanner Services- These are used to generate data on volume.

They collect data for Institutions from

    iv.   Whole sellers

    v.   Retailers, and

vi.   Industrial Firms

Various syndicate services are Operations Research Group (ORG) and The Indian Marketing Research Bureau (IMRB).

Importance of Syndicate Services

Syndicate services are becoming popular since the constraints of decision making are changing and we need more of specific decision-making in the light of changing environment. Also Syndicate services are able to provide information to the industries at a low unit cost.

Disadvantages of Syndicate Services

The information provided is not exclusive. A number of research agencies provide customized services which suits the requirement of each individual organization.

d. International Organization- These includes

i.   The International Labour Organization (ILO)- It publishes data on the total and active population, employment, unemployment, wages and consumer prices

ii.   The Organization for Economic Co-operation and development (OECD)- It publishes data on foreign trade, industry, food, transport, and science and technology.

iii. The International Monetary Fund (IMA)- It publishes reports on national and international foreign exchange regulations.

Brand Management - Meaning and Important Concepts

Brand management begins with having a thorough knowledge of the term "brand". It includes developing a promise, making that promise and maintaining it. It means defining the brand, positioning the brand, and delivering the brand. Brand management is nothing but an art of creating and sustaining the brand. Branding makes customers committed to your business. A strong brand differentiates your products from the competitors. It gives a quality image to your business.

Brand management includes managing the tangible and intangible characteristics of brand. In case of product brands, the tangibles include the product itself, price, packaging, etc. While in case of service brands, the tangibles include the customers' experience. The intangibles include emotional connections with the product / service.

Branding is assembling of various marketing mix medium into a whole so as to give you an identity. It is nothing but capturing your customers mind with your brand name. It gives an image of an experienced, huge and reliable business.

It is all about capturing the niche market for your product / service and about creating a confidence in the current and prospective customers' minds that you are the unique solution to their problem.

The aim of branding is to convey brand message vividly, create customer loyalty, persuade the buyer for the product, and establish an emotional connectivity with the customers. Branding forms customer perceptions about the product. It should raise customer expectations about the product. The primary aim of branding is to create differentiation.

Strong brands reduce customers' perceived monetary, social and safety risks in buying goods/services. The customers can better imagine the intangible goods with the help of brand name. Strong brand organizations have a high market share. The brand should be given good support so that it can sustain itself in long run. It is essential to manage all brands and build brand equity over a period of time. Here comes importance and usefulness of brand management. Brand management helps in building a corporate image. A brand manager has to oversee overall brand performance. A successful brand can only be created if the brand management system is competent. Following are the important concepts of brand management:

✓ Definition of Brand

✓ Brand Name

✓ Brand Attributes

✓ Brand Positioning

✓ Brand Identity

✓ Sources of Brand Identity

✓ Brand Image

✓ Brand Identity vs Brand Image

✓ Brand Personality

✓ Brand Awareness

✓ Brand Loyalty

✓ Brand Association

✓ Building a Brand

✓ Brand Equity

✓ Brand Equity & Customer Equity

✓ Brand Extension

✓ Co-branding

Understanding Brand - What is a Brand ?

Brands are different from products in a way that brands are "what the consumers buy", while products are "what concern/companies make". Brand is an accumulation of emotional and functional associations. Brand is a promise that the product will perform as per customer's expectations. It shapes customer's expectations about the product. Brands usually have a trademark which protects them from use by others. A brand gives particular information about the organization, good or service, differentiating it from others in marketplace. Brand carries an assurance about the characteristics that make the product or service unique. A strong brand is a means of making people aware of what the company represents and what are it's offerings.

To a consumer, brand means and signifies:

- Source of product
- Delegating responsibility to the manufacturer of product
- Lower risk
- Less search cost
- Quality symbol
- Deal or pact with the product manufacturer
- Symbolic device

Brands simplify consumers purchase decision. Over a period of time, consumers discover the brands which satisfy their need. If the consumers recognize a particular brand and have knowledge about it, they make quick purchase decision and save lot of time. Also, they save search costs for product. Consumers remain committed and loyal to a brand as long as they believe and have an implicit understanding that the brand will continue meeting their expectations and perform in the desired manner consistently. As long as the consumers get benefits and satisfaction from consumption of the product, they will more likely continue to buy that brand. Brands also play a crucial role in signifying certain product features to consumers.

To a seller, brand means and signifies:

- Basis of competitive advantage
- Way of bestowing products with unique associations
- Way of identification to easy handling
- Way of legal protection of products' unique traits/features
- Sign of quality to satisfied customer
- Means of financial returns

A brand, in short, can be defined as a seller's promise to provide consistently a unique set of characteristics, advantages, and services to the buyers/consumers. It is a name, term, sign, symbol or a combination of all these planned to differentiate the goods/services of one seller or group of sellers from those of competitors. Some examples of well known brands are Mc Donald's', Mercedes-Benz, Sony, Coca Cola, Kingfisher, etc.

A brand connects the four crucial elements of an enterprise- customers, employees, management and shareholders. Brand is nothing but an assortment of memories in customers mind. Brand represents values, ideas and even personality. It is a set of functional, emotional and rational associations and benefits which have occupied target market's mind. Associations are nothing but the images and symbols associated with the brand or brand benefits, such as, The Nike Swoosh, The Nokia sound, etc. Benefits are the basis for purchase decision.

Brand Name

Brand name is one of the brand elements which helps the customers to identify and differentiate one product from another. It should be chosen very carefully as it captures the key theme of a product in an efficient and economical manner. It can easily be noticed and its meaning can be stored and triggered in the memory instantly. Choice of a brand name requires a lot of research. Brand names are not necessarily associated with the product. For instance, brand names can be based on places (Air India, British Airways), animals or birds (Dove soap, Puma), people (Louise Phillips, Allen Solly). In some instances, the company name is used for all products (General Electric, LG).

Features of a Good Brand Name

A good brand name should have following characteristics:

1. It should be unique / distinctive (for instance- Kodak, Mustang)

2. It should be extendable.

3. It should be easy to pronounce, identified and memorized. (For instance-Tide)

4. It should give an idea about product's qualities and benefits (For instance- Swift, Quickfix, Lipguard).

5. It should be easily convertible into foreign languages.

6. It should be capable of legal protection and registration.

7. It should suggest product/service category (For instance Newsweek).

8. It should indicate concrete qualities (For instance Firebird).

9. It should not portray bad/wrong meanings in other categories. (For instance NOVA is a poor name for a car

to be sold in Spanish country, because in Spanish it means "doesn't go").

Process of Selecting a renowned and successful Brand Name

1. Define the objectives of branding in terms of six criterions - descriptive, suggestive, compound, classical, arbitrary and fanciful. It Is essential to recognize the role of brand within the corporate branding strategy and the relation of brand to other brand and products. It is also essential to understand the role of brand within entire marketing program as well as a detailed description of niche market must be considered.

2. Generation of multiple names - Any potential source of names can be used; organization, management and employees, current or potential customers, agencies and professional consultants.

3. Screening of names on the basis of branding objectives and marketing considerations so as to have a more synchronized list - The brand names must not have connotations, should be easily pronounceable, should meet the legal requirements etc.

4. Gathering more extensive details on each of the finalized names - There should be extensive international legal search done. These searches are at times done on a sequential basis because of the expense involved.

5. Conducting consumer research - Consumer research is often conducted so as to confirm management expectations as to the remembrance and meaningfulness of the brand names. The features of the product, its price and promotion may be shown to the consumers so that they understand the purpose of the brand name and the manner in which it will be used. Consumers can be shown actual 3-D packages as well as animated advertising or boards. Several samples of consumers must be surveyed depending on the niche market involved.

6. On the basis of the above steps, management can finalize the brand name that maximizes the organization's branding and marketing objectives and then formally register the brand name.

Brand Attributes

Brand Attributes portray a company's brand characteristics. They signify the basic nature of brand. Brand attributes are a bundle of features that highlight the physical and personality aspects of the brand. Attributes are developed through images, actions, or presumptions. Brand attributes help in creating brand identity.

A strong brand must have following attributes:

1. **Relevancy-** A strong brand must be relevant. It must meet people's expectations and should perform the way they want it to. A good job must be done to persuade consumers to buy the product; else inspite of your product being unique, people will not buy it.

2. **Consistency-** A consistent brand signifies what the brand stands for and builds customers trust in brand. A consistent brand is where the company communicates message in a way that does not deviate from the core brand proposition.

3. **Proper positioning-**A strong brand should be positioned so that it makes a place in target audience mind and they prefer it over other brands.

4. **Sustainable-** A strong brand makes a business competitive. A sustainable brand drives an organization towards innovation and success. Example of sustainable brand is Marks and Spencer's.

5. **Credibility-** A strong brand should do what it promises. The way you communicate your brand to the audience/ customers should be realistic. It should not fail to deliver what it promises. Do not exaggerate as customers want to believe in the promises you make to them.

6. **Inspirational-** A strong brand should transcend/ inspire the category it is famous for. For example- Nike transcendent Jersey Polo Shirt.

7. **Uniqueness-** A strong brand should be different and unique. It should set you apart from other competitors in market.

8. **Appealing-** A strong brand should be attractive. Customers should be attracted by the promise you make and by the value you deliver.

Brand Positioning - Definition and Concept

Brand positioning refers to "target consumer's" reason to buy your brand in preference to others. It is ensures that all brand activity has a common aim; is guided, directed and delivered by the brand's benefits/reasons to buy; and it focusses at all points of contact with the consumer.

Brand positioning must make sure that:

- Is it unique/distinctive vs. competitors ?

- Is it significant and encouraging to the niche market ?

- Is it appropriate to all major geographic markets and businesses ?

- Is the proposition validated with unique, appropriate and original products ?

- Is it sustainable - can it be delivered constantly across all points of contact with the consumer ?

- Is it helpful for organization to achieve its financial goals ?

- Is it able to support and boost up the organization ?

In order to create a distinctive place in the market, a niche market has to be carefully chosen and a differential advantage must be created in their mind. Brand positioning is a medium through which an organization can portray it's customers what it wants to achieve for them and what it wants to mean to them. Brand positioning forms customer's views and opinions.

Brand Positioning can be defined as an activity of creating a brand offer in such a manner that it occupies a distinctive place and value in the target customer's mind. For instance-Kotak Mahindra positions itself in the customer's mind as one entity- "Kotak "- which can provide customized and one-stop solution for all their financial services needs. It has an unaided top of mind recall. It intends to stay with the proposition of "Think Investments, Think Kotak". The positioning you choose for your brand will be influenced by the competitive stance you want to adopt.

Brand Positioning involves identifying and determining points of similarity and difference to ascertain the right brand identity and to create a proper brand image. Brand Positioning is the key of marketing strategy. A strong brand positioning directs marketing strategy by explaining the brand details, the uniqueness of brand and it's similarity with the competitive brands, as well as the reasons for buying and using that specific brand. Positioning is the base for developing and increasing the required knowledge and perceptions of the customers. It is the single feature that sets your service apart from your competitors. For instance- Kingfisher stands for youth and excitement. It represents brand in full flight.

There are various positioning errors, such as-

1. **Under positioning-** This is a scenario in which the customer's have a blurred and unclear idea of the brand.

2. **Over positioning-** This is a scenario in which the customers have too limited a awareness of the brand.

3. **Confused positioning-** This is a scenario in which the customers have a confused opinion of the brand.

4. **Double Positioning-** This is a scenario in which customers do not accept the claims of a brand.

Brand Identity - Definition and Concept

Brand identity stems from an organization, i.e., an organization is responsible for creating a distinguished product with unique characteristics. It is how an organization seeks to identify itself. It represents how an organization wants to be perceived in the market. An organization communicates its identity to the consumers through its branding and marketing strategies. A brand is unique due to its identity. Brand identity includes following elements - Brand vision, brand culture, positioning, personality, relationships, and presentations.

Brand identity is a bundle of mental and functional associations with the brand. Associations are not "reasons-to-buy" but provide familiarity and differentiation that's not replicable getting it. These associations can include signature tune(for example - Britannia "ting-ting-ta-ding"), trademark colours (for example - Blue colour with Pepsi), logo (for example - Nike), tagline (for example - Apple's tagline is "Think different"),etc.

Brand identity is the total proposal/promise that an organization makes to consumers. The brand can be perceived as a product, a personality, a set of values, and a position it occupies in consumer's minds. Brand identity is all that an organization wants the brand to be considered as. It is a feature linked with a specific company, product, service or individual. It is a way of externally expressing a brand to the world.

Brand identity is the noticeable elements of a brand (for instance - Trademark colour, logo, name, symbol) that identify and differentiates a brand in target audience mind. It is a crucial means to grow your company's brand.

Brand identity is the aggregation of what all you (i.e. an organization) do. It is an organizations mission, personality, promise to the consumers and competitive advantages. It includes the thinking, feelings and expectations of the target market/consumers. It is a means of identifying and distinguishing an organization from another. An organization having unique brand identity have improved brand awareness, motivated team of employees who feel proud working in a well branded organization, active buyers, and corporate style. Brand identity leads to brand loyalty, brand preference, high credibility, good prices and good financial returns. It helps the organization to express to the customers and the target market the kind of organization it is. It assures the customers again that you are who you say you are. It establishes an immediate connection between the organization and consumers. Brand identity should be sustainable. It is crucial so that the consumers instantly correlate with your product/service.

Brand identity should be futuristic, i.e, it should reveal the associations aspired for the brand. It should reflect the durable qualities of a brand. Brand identity is a basic means of consumer recognition and represents the brand's distinction from it's competitors.

Sources of Brand Identity

1. **SYMBOLS-** Symbols help customers memorize organization's products and services. They help us correlate positive attributes that bring us closer and make it convenient for us to purchase those products and services. Symbols emphasize our brand expectations and shape corporate images. Symbols become a key component of brand equity and help in differentiating the

brand characteristics. Symbols are easier to memorize than the brand names as they are visual images. These can include logos, people, geometric shapes, cartoon images, anything. For instance, Marlboro has its famous cowboy, Pillsbury has its Poppin' Fresh doughboy, Duracell has its bunny rabbit, Mc Donald has Ronald, Fed Ex has an arrow, and Nike's swoosh. All these symbols help us remember the brands associated with them.

Brand symbols are strong means to attract attention and enhance brand personalities by making customers like them. It is feasible to learn the relationship between symbol and brand if the symbol is reflective/representative of the brand. For instance, the symbol of LG symbolize the world, future, youth, humanity, and technology. Also, it represents LG's efforts to keep close relationships with their customers.

2. **LOGOS-** A logo is a unique graphic or symbol that represents a company, product, service, or other entity. It represents an organization very well and make the customers well-acquainted with the company. It is due to logo that customers form an image for the

product/service in mind. Adidas's "Three Stripes" is a famous brand identified by it's corporate logo.

Features of a good logo are :

   a. It should be simple.

   b. It should be distinguished/unique. It should differentiate itself.

   c. It should be functional so that it can be used widely.

   d. It should be effective, i.e., it must have an impact on the intended audience.

   e. It should be memorable.

   f. It should be easily identifiable in full colours, limited colour palettes, or in black and white.

   g. It should be a perfect reflection/representation of the organization.

   h. It should be easy to correlate by the customers and should develop customers trust in the organization.

   i. It should not loose it's integrity when transferred on fabric or any other material.

   j. It should portray company's values, mission and objectives.

The elements of a logo are:

11. Logotype - It can be a simple or expanded name. Examples of logotypes including only the name are Kellogg's, Hyatt, etc.

12. Icon - It is a name or visual symbol that communicates a market position. For example-LIC 'hands', UTI 'kalash'.

13. Slogan - It is best way of conveying company's message to the consumers. For instance- Nike's slogan "Just Do It".

TRADEMARKS- Trademark is a unique symbol, design, or any form of identification that helps people recognize a brand. A renowned brand has a popular trademark and that helps consumers purchase quality products. The goodwill of the dealer/maker of the product also enhances by use of trademark. Trademark totally indicates the commercial source of product/service. Trademark contribute in brand equity formation of a brand. Trademark name should be original. A trademark is chosen by the following symbols:

™ (denotes unregistered trademark, that is, a mark used to promote or brand goods);

SM (denotes unregistered service mark)

® (denotes registered trademark).

Registration of trademark is essential in some countries to give exclusive rights to it. Without adequate trademark protection, brand names can become legally declared generic. Generic names are never protectable as was the case with Vaseline, escalator and thermos.

Some guidelines for trademark protection are as follows:

xiv.   Go for formal trademark registration.

xv.   Never use trademark as a noun or verb. Always use it as an adjective.

xvi.   Use correct trademark spelling.

xvii.   Challenge each misuse of trademark, specifically by competitors in market.

xviii.   Capitalize first letter of trademark. If a trademark appears in point, ensure that it stands out from surrounding text.

Brand Image

Brand image is the current view of the customers about a brand. It can be defined as a unique bundle of associations within the minds of target customers. It signifies what the brand presently stands for. It is a set of beliefs held about a specific brand. In short, it is nothing but the consumers' perception about the product. It is the manner in which a specific brand is positioned in the market. Brand image conveys emotional value and not just a mental image. Brand image is nothing but an organization's character. It is an accumulation of contact and observation by people external to an organization. It should highlight an organization's mission and vision to all. The main elements of positive brand image are- unique logo reflecting organization's image, slogan describing organization's business in brief and brand identifier supporting the key values.

Brand image is the overall impression in consumers' mind that is formed from all sources. Consumers develop various associations with the brand. Based on these associations, they form brand image. An image is formed about the brand on the basis of subjective perceptions of associations bundle that the consumers have about the brand. Volvo is associated with safety. Toyota is associated with reliability.

The idea behind brand image is that the consumer is not purchasing just the product/service but also the image associated with that product/service. Brand images should be positive, unique and instant. Brand images can be strengthened using brand communications like advertising, packaging, word of mouth publicity, other promotional tools, etc.

Brand image develops and conveys the product's character in a unique manner different from its competitor's image. The brand image consists of various associations in consumers' mind - attributes, benefits and attributes. Brand attributes are the functional and mental connections with the brand that the customers have. They can be specific or conceptual. Benefits are the rationale for the purchase decision. There are three types of benefits: Functional benefits - what do you do better (than others),emotional benefits - how do you make me feel better (than others), and rational benefits/support - why do I believe you(more than others). Brand attributes are consumers overall assessment of a brand. Brand image has not to be created, but is automatically formed. The brand image includes products' appeal, ease of use, functionality, fame, and overall value. Brand image is actually brand content. When the consumers purchase the product, they are also purchasing it's image. Brand image is the objective and mental feedback of the consumers when they purchase a product. Positive brand image is exceeding the customers expectations. Positive brand image enhances the goodwill and brand value of an organization.

To sum up, "Brand image" is the customer's net extract from the brand.

Brand Identity vs Brand Image

	Brand Identity	Brand Image
1	Brand identity develops from the source or the company.	Brand image is perceived by the receiver or the consumer.
2	Brand message is tied together in terms of brand identity.	Brand message is untied by the consumer in the form of brand image.
3	The general meaning of brand identity is "who you really are?"	The general meaning of brand image is "How market perceives you?"
4	It's nature is that it is substance oriented or strategic.	It's nature is that it is appearance oriented or tactical.
5	Brand identity symbolizes	Brand image symbolizes

	firms' reality.	perception of consumers
6	Brand identity represents "your desire".	Brand image represents "others view"
7	It is enduring.	It is superficial.
8	Identity is looking ahead.	Image is looking back.
9	Identity is active.	Image is passive.
10	It signifies "where you want to be".	It signifies "what you have got".
11	It is total promise that a company makes to consumers.	It is total consumers' perception about the brand.

Focus on shaping your brand identity, brand image will follow.

What is Brand Personality ?

Brand personality is the way a brand speaks and behaves. It means assigning human personality traits/characteristics to a brand so as to achieve differentiation. These characteristics signify brand behaviour through both individuals representing the brand (i.e. it's employees) as well as through advertising, packaging, etc. When brand image or brand identity is expressed in terms of human traits, it is called brand personality. For instance - Allen Solley brand speaks the personality and makes the individual who wears it stand apart from the crowd. Infosys represents uniqueness, value, and intellectualism.

Brand personality is nothing but personification of brand. A brand is expressed either as a personality who embodies these personality traits (For instance - Shahrukh Khan and Airtel, John Abraham and Castrol) or distinct personality traits (For instance - Dove as honest, feminist and optimist; Hewlett Packard brand represents accomplishment, competency and influence). Brand personality is the result of all the consumer's experiences with the brand. It is unique and long lasting.

Brand personality must be differentiated from brand image, in sense that, while brand image denote the tangible (physical and functional) benefits and attributes of a brand, brand personality indicates emotional associations of the brand. If brand image is comprehensive brand according to consumers' opinion, brand personality is that aspect of comprehensive brand which generates it's emotional character and associations in consumers' mind.

Brand personality develops brand equity. It sets the brand attitude. It is a key input into the look and feel of any communication or marketing activity by the brand. It helps in gaining thorough knowledge of customers feelings about the brand. Brand personality differentiates among brands specifically when they are alike in many attributes. For instance - Sony versus Panasonic. Brand personality is used to make the brand strategy lively, i.e, to implement brand strategy. Brand personality indicates the kind of relationship a customer has with the brand. It is a means by which a customer communicates his own identity.

Brand personality and celebrity should supplement each other. Trustworthy celebrity ensures immediate awareness, acceptability and optimism towards the brand. This will influence consumers' purchase decision and also create brand loyalty. For instance - Bollywood actress Priyanka Chopra is brand ambassador for J.Hampstead, international line of premium shirts.

Brand personality not only includes the personality features/characteristics, but also the demographic features like age, gender or class and psychographic features. Personality traits are what the brand exists for.

What is Brand Awareness ?

Brand awareness is the probability that consumers are familiar about the life and availability of the product. It is the degree to which consumers precisely associate the brand with the specific product. It is measured as ratio of niche market that has former knowledge of brand. Brand awareness includes both brand recognition as well as brand recall. Brand recognition is the ability of consumer to recognize prior knowledge of brand when they are asked questions about that brand or when they are shown that specific brand, i.e., the consumers can clearly differentiate the brand as having being earlier noticed or heard. While brand recall is the potential of customer to recover a brand from his memory when given the product class/category, needs satisfied by that category or buying scenario as a signal. In other words, it refers that consumers should correctly recover brand from the memory when given a clue or he can recall the specific brand when the product category is mentioned. It is generally easier to recognize a brand rather than recall it from the memory.

Brand awareness is improved to the extent to which brand names are selected that is simple and easy to pronounce or spell; known and expressive; and unique as well as distinct. For instance - Coca Cola has come to be known as Coke.

There are two types of brand awareness:

1. **Aided awareness-** This means that on mentioning the product category, the customers recognize your brand from the lists of brands shown.

2. **Top of mind awareness (Immediate brand recall)-** This means that on mentioning the product category, the first brand that customer recalls from his mind is your brand.

The relative importance of brand recall and recognition will rely on the degree to which consumers make product-related decisions with the brand present or not. For instance - In a store, brand recognition is more crucial as the brand will be physically present. In a scenario where brands are not physically present, brand recall is more significant (as in case of services and online brands).

Building brand awareness is essential for building brand equity. It includes use of various renowned channels of promotion such as advertising, word of mouth publicity, social media like blogs, sponsorships, launching events, etc. To create brand awareness, it is important to create reliable brand image, slogans and taglines. The brand message to be communicated should also be consistent. Strong brand awareness leads to high sales and high market share. Brand awareness can be regarded as a means through which consumers become acquainted and familiar with a brand and recognize that brand.

Brand Loyalty

Brand Loyalty is a scenario where the consumer fears purchasing and consuming product from another brand which he does not trust. It is measured through methods like word of mouth publicity, repetitive buying, price sensitivity, commitment, brand trust, customer satisfaction, etc. Brand loyalty is the extent to which a consumer constantly buys the same brand within a product category. The consumers remain loyal to a specific brand as long as it is available. They do not buy from other suppliers within the product category. Brand loyalty exists when the consumer feels that the brand consists of right product characteristics and quality at right price. Even if the other brands are available at cheaper price or superior quality, the brand loyal consumer will stick to his brand.

Brand loyal consumers are the foundation of an organization. Greater loyalty levels lead to less marketing expenditure because the brand loyal customers promote the brand positively. Also, it acts as a means of launching and introducing more products that are targeted at same customers at less expenditure. It also restrains new competitors in the market. Brand loyalty is a key component of brand equity.

Brand loyalty can be developed through various measures such as quick service, ensuring quality products, continuous improvement, wide distribution network, etc. When consumers are brand loyal they love "you" for being "you", and they will minutely consider any other alternative brand as a replacement. Examples of brand loyalty can be seen in US where true Apple customers have the brand's logo tattooed onto their bodies. Similarly in Finland, Nokia customers remained loyal to Nokia because they admired the design of the handsets or because of user- friendly menu system used by Nokia phones.

Brand loyalty can be defined as relative possibility of customer shifting to another brand in case there is a change in product's features, price or quality. As brand loyalty increases, customers will respond less to competitive moves and actions. Brand loyal customers remain committed to the brand, are willing to pay higher price for that brand, and will promote their brand always. A company having brand loyal customers will have greater sales, less marketing and advertising costs, and best pricing. This is because the brand loyal customers are less reluctant to shift to other brands, respond less to price changes and self- promote the brand as they perceive that their brand have unique value which is not provided by other competitive brands.

Brand loyalty is always developed post purchase. To develop brand loyalty, an organization should know their niche market, target them, support their product, ensure easy access of their product, provide customer satisfaction, bring constant innovation in their product and offer schemes on their product so as to ensure that customers repeatedly purchase the product.

Brand Promise - Our brand is a promise of what we deliver

Brand evokes the responses. There are many people who love their Apple iPod or love their car etc. There are certain feelings that come to your mind when you think about your favorite brands. People expect that these brands should demonstrate brand promises every time whenever they are, encountered. Inconsistencies in the performance of services can lead to damage in further relations. This can cause a customer to select some other brand.

Brand promise is what you say to the customer and what is to be delivered. If you are not able to meet the expectations of the customer, your business will either flounder or die. If you are not able to deliver the brand promise you will not be able to meet the expectations that have been created in the customers mind.

There are three major mistakes that the business leaders make while executing and developing the brand promise:

- The first mistake is when you refuse to recognize the customer expectations that are created in customers mind before it comes in contact with that particular brand. The customers are very easily able to realize your brand promise by the business you are dealing with. For example, if you have a gourmet restaurant then the customers will have a image in their mind that it will different from the local restaurant. This is one of the major reason, why one should work for every smallest detail. For example, the image of a gourmet restaurant does not include plastic menus or paper placemats.

✓ The second major mistake is to implement a system which gives a negative experience to the customer. Business leaders work on creating efficient results for saving time and money. Human beings are self-centered creatures with a thought in their mind to save money and time for us. For example, a customers asks do you accept credit card? Do you accept all credit cards or only master card and visa? If you don't accept these cards, does it make any difference in the cost? Its just that you are losing sales. Then what are the other services you are giving to the customer in place which is the attraction for the customers. Any small inconvenience which will force the customer to say that "you are not completely service oriented" and encourages the customer to some other brand.

✓ The third major mistake is that when you are not able to hire the best candidate. You easily hire anyone who applies and don't even put some efforts to train them gives a really terrible experience to the customers. Brand promises are delivered by the staff. If your goal is to be a business leader you will invest time to train the staff. If you select a person who is very polite and does not even know how to dress up for an interview then you competition should send a thank you card for all the business you will send his way.

People who want to become the business leader understand they are a great product brands. They are authentic, dependable and reliable. Their icon is their name. Delivering the best of themselves is their brand promise. Do you want to become winner at working? Then, deliver the brand promise.

Steps in Building a Brand Name Product or Service

At times, organizations are often inspired by a variety of ideas to create products and services which can be offered locally or globally. Generally, such products or services require the establishment of a brand or company name. Often these brands include both logo and lettering and can do a long way in advertising such products or services. Therefore, one of the most important steps in building a Brand is decide upon a brand name for the product or service one wishes to sell. Branding is a process that allows an individual or a group of individuals the ability to provide a <u>brand image</u> and lettering to an idea. Upon doing so, one has a better chance of selling such items to a broader audience whether that be on a local or global level. Therefore, while the old adage "nothing happens until somebody sells something," still stands true to some extent, at times almost seems as if the process of advertising and branding has overtaken the desire to sell.

Although branding generally identifies the company and philosophies behind same, it can also be representative of those working for such a company. This is a good thing as it generates the right type of audience to the product or service being sold based on personal relationships with those running the company. Therefore, benefiting both the organizations selling the branded product or service and the dealers buying same.

One of the most important steps in selling any product or service is the belief one holds in relation to the item. Therefore, only those who strongly believe in the products and services offered by the company are going to be good at selling same. Otherwise, one may want to work from an advertising or graphic artist perspective in relation to advertising rather than sales when it comes to time to market same.

Another step is to build a brand that maintains <u>loyalty</u> with its customer base and has a strong customer service department. For, having such a department in today's world where one is both experienced and knowledgeable when it comes to helping others can be a rare find. So, companies who represent oneself has having a strong customer base and even stronger customer service department are often more successful than those who do not.

A very important step in marketing a brand is to identify the target audience before creating the logo and lettering in relation to marketing. This is because different age groups react differently to a variety of logo and lettering especially as so much is misrepresented by a variety of gangs and others using such material inappropriately. Therefore, if one can define the brand name, logo and lettering and present same to a marketing research review panel or the like, one may be able to gain a better understanding of which audience one needs to direct their product or service to in order to create the most sales.

Still, if one can communicate the use of their product or service clearly, establish trust within the community, be that locally or globally, aim marketing at the right audience, build a base of buyers and customer loyalty and offer great customer service, then one is on their way to not only creating and advertising an excellent brand but selling one as well.

Therefore, when looking for steps in building a brand, there are many steps which one can complete to help make the creation of such brand an easier task. These include, knowing your audience, building your brand, finding a great logo and lettering to represent same, targeting the appropriate audience and placing a number of ads in as many online and offline advertising venues one can find. For, after doing so, one may just find that they are selling even more products and services than one had ever dreamed possible.

Brand Extension - Meaning, Advantages and Disadvantages

Brand Extension is the use of an established brand name in new product categories. This new category to which the brand is extended can be related or unrelated to the existing product categories. A renowned/successful brand helps an organization to launch products in new categories more easily.

For instance, Nike's brand core product is shoes. But it is now extended to sunglasses, soccer balls, basketballs, and golf equipments. An existing brand that gives rise to a brand extension is referred to as parent brand. If the customers of the new business have values and aspirations synchronizing/matching those of the core business, and if these values and aspirations are embodied in the brand, it is likely to be accepted by customers in the new business.

Extending a brand outside its core product category can be beneficial in a sense that it helps evaluating product category opportunities, identifies resource requirements, lowers risk, and measures brand's relevance and appeal.

Brand extension may be successful or unsuccessful.

Instances where brand extension has been a success are-Wipro which was originally into computers has extended into shampoo, powder, and soap.

i. Mars is no longer a famous bar only, but an ice-cream, chocolate drink and a slab of chocolate.

Instances where brand extension has been a failure are-

i. In case of new Coke, Coca Cola has forgotten what the core brand was meant to stand for. It thought that taste was the only factor that consumer cared about. It was wrong. The time and money spent on research on new Coca Cola could not evaluate the deep emotional attachment to the original Coca- Cola.

ii. Rasna Ltd. - Is among the famous soft drink companies in India. But when it tried to move away from its niche, it hasn't had much success. When it experimented with fizzy fruit drink "Oranjolt", the brand bombed even before it could take off. Oranjolt was a fruit drink in which carbonates were used as preservative. It didn't work out because it was out of synchronization with retail practices. Oranjolt need to be refrigerated and it also faced quality problems. It has a shelf life of three-four weeks, while other soft- drinks assured life of five months.

Advantages of Brand Extension

Brand Extension has following advantages:

1. It makes acceptance of new product easy.

   a. It increases brand image.

   b. The risk perceived by the customers reduces.

   c. The likelihood of gaining distribution and trial increases. An established brand name increases consumer interest and willingness to try new product having the established brand name.

d. The efficiency of promotional expenditure increases. Advertising, selling and promotional costs are reduced. There are economies of scale as advertising for core brand and its extension reinforces each other.

e. Cost of developing new brand is saved.

f. Consumers can now seek for a variety.

g. There are packaging and labeling efficiencies.

h. The expense of introductory and follow up marketing programs is reduced.

2. There are feedback benefits to the parent brand and the organization.

a. The image of parent brand is enhanced.

b. It revives the brand.

c. It allows subsequent extension.

d. Brand meaning is clarified.

e. It increases market coverage as it brings new customers into brand franchise.

f. Customers associate original/core brand to new product, hence they also have quality associations.

Disadvantages of Brand Extension

1. Brand extension in unrelated markets may lead to loss of reliability if a brand name is extended too far. An organization must research the product categories in which the established brand name will work.

2. There is a risk that the new product may generate implications that damage the image of the core/original brand.

3. There are chances of less awareness and trial because the management may not provide enough investment for the introduction of new product assuming that the spin-off effects from the original brand name will compensate.

4. If the brand extensions have no advantage over competitive brands in the new category, then it will fail.

Brand Extension - A Success or Failure ?

Brand management has become quite a challenge for brand managers as well as the Organizations today. Intense competition and the decreasing product life of a brand add further dimensions to the brand management problem. Brand managers by and large opt for brand extensions now days. You can check any shelf in the super market and you will see variants of the same brand occupying the shelf space. This is true in all cases be it with a soft drink brand leader like Coke to a cream, shampoo or toiletry.

Brand managers are always under pressure to grow the market share and increase revenue. Under constant pressure and intense competition, they find it easier to bring out brand extensions in order to provide continual change and an increased value perception to the consumers. Brand extensions also help them to capture the niche segments in the market that have not be covered by the parent brand. On the part of the management, brand extensions prove to help in maximizing capacity utilization and stretching resources to the maximum.

However, the question that bothers every brand manager is whether such brand extension is good for the parent brand or whether it is a mistake that one is committing in the long run. There is no straight answer to this question. In some cases, brands like GE, Proctor & Gamble, Spencer's etc have been hugely successful in making foray into new businesses using the parent brand and stretching the brand. Brand extensions too have worked well for brands like Nivea, Dove and Loreal etc. In many cases, the brand extensions and stretching exercises have failed too.

There is definitely a case for brand extensions in the market for various reasons. There is nothing wrong in a firm exploiting the brand image or brand value when they have strived to build the parent brand over a period of time. Economically too it makes sense for the company to resort to brand extension which is far cheaper than introducing and promoting a new brand. If successful, brand extensions can help strengthen the parent brand as well as capture the niche market segments no doubt.

However, the thinking behind the brand extension and the strategy is what makes the brand extension a failure or a success. In cases where the brand extension is planned to auger short term revenue, it may not withstand the test of times. The danger of brand extension is something that should be accounted for before jumping into brand extensions. The failure of a brand extension can affect the perception of the consumers with regard to the parent brand and damage the brand value. In Some cases, the brand extension products may not generate new revenue but eat into the parent brand's market share itself.

What works for brand extension is difficult to say. Depending upon the product, one can perhaps map the market and arrive at a good judgment. Categories like biscuits, soft drinks, chewing gum, sauces and jams etc generally do well with brand extensions. The same does not hold good in terms of all products.

Branding experts opine that though there is no guaranteed formulae for success in brand extensions, when the same is carried out as a part of a well identified and planned strategy, it can be successful. A well identified and planned strategy involves identifying the core brand value and perception and building brand extension by retaining the same values but delivering increased value through brand extension. Co-branding - Meaning, Types and Advantages and Disadvantages

What is Co-branding

Co branding is the utilization of two or more brands to name a new product. The ingredient brands help each other to achieve their aims. The overall synchronization between the brand pair and the new product has to be kept in mind. Example of co-branding - Citibank co-branded with MTV to launch a co-branded debit card. This card is beneficial to customers who can avail benefits at specific outlets called MTV Citibank club.

Types of Co-branding

Co-branding is of two types: Ingredient co-branding and Composite co-branding.

1. Ingredient co-branding implies using a renowned brand as an element in the production of another renowned brand. This deals with creation of brand equity for materials and parts that are contained within other products. The ingredient/constituent brand is subordinate to the primary brand. For instance - Dell computers has co-branding strategy with Intel processors. The brands which are ingredients are usually the company's biggest buyers or present suppliers. The ingredient brand should be unique. It should either be a major brand or should be protected by a patent. Ingredient co-branding leads to better quality products, superior promotions, more access to distribution channel and greater profits. The seller of ingredient brand enjoys long-term customer relations. The brand manufacture can benefit by having a competitive advantage and the retailer can benefit by enjoying a promotional help from ingredient brand.

2. Composite co-branding refers to use of two renowned brand names in a way that they can collectively offer a

distinct product/ service that could not be possible individually. The success of composite branding depends upon the favourability of the ingredient brands and also upon the extent on complementarities between them.

Advantages and Disadvantages of Co-branding

Co-branding has various advantages, such as - risk-sharing, generation of royalty income, more sales income, greater customer trust on the product, wide scope due to joint advertising, technological benefits, better product image by association with another renowned brand, and greater access to new sources of finance. But co-branding is not free from limitations. Co-branding may fail when the two products have different market and are entirely different. If there is difference in visions and missions of the two companies, then also composite branding may fail. Co-branding may affect partner brands in adverse manner. If the customers associate any adverse experience with a constituent brand, then it may damage the total brand equity.

What is Brand Value ?

Branding has emerged as a corporate strategy in the recent times. All business organizations in all sectors have embraced the strategy of building their identity through their corporate brands besides the product related brands. Branding is definitely a marketing strategy. However the strategy of investing into brand building and managing the reputation of the corporate brand goes beyond marketing. Branding is considered to be a strategy that is driven and managed by the CEO or the organization along with the senior management as well as marketing heads. Over the recent years, we see new concepts of brand value, brand power and brand equity etc. being coined and measured.

If marketing professionals found it difficult to justify and obtain sanctions for the brand promotional activity, today they no longer need to worry. Brand value and expenses towards brand building have become an accepted part of the balance sheet. Capitalizing the brand value and the expenses towards meeting the brand promotion are budgeted and accounted for in the balance sheets and in many cases the ROI of a brand is also calculated to reflect the brand value status over time.

Brand management has gained prominence in recent times. The fact that we have global brands that have been well established for over fifty years goes on to prove the fact that brands certainly have the power to make or break in the markets. Goodyear, Coco Cola, Gillette, Nestle, Kelloggs,

Schweppes, Brooke bond etc have been around for a very long time and have gained certain brand power to drive growth through brand reputation and relationship with the consumers. Marketers have realized the growing power of brands and have begun to nurture the brand image and cultivate value through brand ambassadors. Most of the lifestyle and luxury brands globally and locally have well known actors and sports persons etc as brand ambassadors. Through the persona of the brand ambassadors, the marketers derive the power to connect with the consumers and build brand loyalty. Realizing the brand power also calls for working on the product quality and continuous modification both in the product as well as in the promotion of brand ambassadors. Building and growing strong brand at a global level calls for the entire organization to be brand oriented. The best example of building and realizing strong brand power and unleashing the brand value is Apple. If you think that the entire world outside is an Apple fan, you are right. But the entire organization within also worship their brand too. All of the strategies, decisions as well as day to day business decisions at all levels are directed towards promotion of and strengthening of the apple brand. The entire organization believes in the brand and all business processes are driven to build the brand and deliver superior customer experience through the brand. Apple as a global brand is perhaps the best example of a successful corporate brand.

As much as the corporate strategy has got to account for the branding strategy, the marketing has also to ensure that they work on the different aspects of the brand packaging, design, etc and keep working on the brand so that it is consistent with the changing times, markets, consumer expectations and taste etc.

The brands have their own value. The market leadership and profitability of a certain product or business is realized through the brand value. Growing the brand power and using the brand value as a driver to increase profitability as well as the market calls for expert management of branding. Maintaining the leadership of a brand calls for strategic planning in the long term perspective.

Brand Value Measurement

Brands have a certain value in the market as well as in the balance sheets of the organization that owns the brand. This is a matter that has been agreed upon by the industry. The accounting of the brand value and the methodology for calculation of the brand value is widely debated. When organizations pay a huge premium or goodwill to acquire a brand, it becomes a strategic decision. However accounting for the premium paid is a matter that is discussed and debated by many in the industry.

No doubt accountants would like to assign a tangible value to every asset owned by the company and brand value paid to acquire a particular brand and the business is also considered to be an asset. One of the systems followed by UK based business organizations is that they capitalize the entire value paid for acquiring the business and the same is depreciated over a period of time.

Interbrand, the branding company has proposed a different method of accounting for the brand value. This method as well as the other methods that are proposed by industry experts take into account the future sales potential of the brand as well as its current market share to arrive at a definitive figure in terms of brand equity or brand power.

Accordingly one of the models followed by the industry accounts for the net profit earned by the brand in the last three consecutive years in terms of value. To this, is added a score that is derived out of measuring certain key factors associated with the brand like brand leadership, market share, trend, loyalty etc. Certain weight age is given to each of the factors and the total score is then converted into a certain value with the help of a multiple that is again derived out of a market study conducted for that particular sector.

Similarly there are several other models and methods that have been proposed by experts in the industry. All of the models use a combination of qualitative and quantitative factors to arrive at a measurable value in terms of Brand Equity. Some of the well known models are Brand Equity Index, Consumer Brand Equity Brand Asset by Longman Moran and Leo Burnett, Conversion Model Equity Monitor etc. The factors included in the above vary from Quality of the brand to Customer attitude, perception, market share, price band, durability etc.

A reasonable model to measure brand equity becomes essential not only for the accountants but for the business Organization that is looking out to buy a brand. Valuation of a brand and fixing the right price or premium for the brand needs a proven methodology and model that can guide the decision making. It is also true that one model cannot satisfy the finance and accounts personnel as well as the business managers, for each one's perceptions and purpose of evaluation is different. When brands are key to the growth and business strategy of the Organizations, the decision makers would definitely need proven and strong models to guide them for decision making. Besides the models they would need to analyze the brand equity from many other points of view of product portfolio, growth potential of the brand to see if a particular brand is the right choice for them. If there exists a strategic synergy between the brand and the buyer's business needs, then the brand value is likely to change and the buyer might find that he is required to pay a premium over and above the perceived brand value. At what price does it make sense to acquire the brand is a decision that is critical to the buyer. Brand value models can certainly aid him in this decision making process.

www.ingramcontent.com/pod-product-compliance
Lightning Source LLC
Chambersburg PA
CBHW080817180526
45168CB00006B/2486